party
with
Sweet Treats

dressed-up goodies
for EVERY occasion

PRAISE FOR PARTY WITH SWEET TREATS

"*Party with Sweet Treats* is full of easy, edible crafts to make your parties the talk of the town!"
—*Barbara Corcoran, real estate mogul and star of the hit television show* Shark Tank

"When I first came across Norene's site, partypinching.com, I thought: This is one talented girl! I didn't think I could pull off anything that resembled one of her cute food creations. Imagine my surprise when I was able to recreate a few of her tiny treats for Halloween in about 15 minutes, using ingredients I found at the drugstore/local grocery store. *Party With Sweet Treats* is a magic wand of a book that can turn any novice sweet-maker into a master confectioner! *Party With Sweet Treats* is the GO-TO hostess gift!"
—*Danneel Ackles, actress and mom*

"Well, Norene has shown us once again that food can and should be FUN! Her creative eye for transform-ing everyday treats into works of art is second to none, and she continues to be a huge source of inspira-tion with her simple-to-reproduce yet genius ideas! If you're looking to inject a dose of fabulousness and a sprinkle of whimsy to your parties and celebrations, then this book is a must read!"
—*Bird, author, designer, and founder of* Bird's Party

"Norene has an amazing gift for transforming store-bought sweets into the most ADORABLE kid-friendly party treats! From seasonal and holiday themes to baby and bridal showers (and more!), this book is filled with crowd-pleasing projects that are sure to make your celebrations that much sweeter!"
—*Melissa Diamond, founder of* MyCakeSchool.com

"In the world of food crafts, Norene is a pioneer. What she can create out of basic ingredients is amazing. I'm always delighted and surprised by how her mind works."
—*Jillian Tohber Leslie,* CatchMyParty.com

"Norene is a STAR at creating amazing treats! Her creativity is mind-boggling—you will ask yourself again and again: How did she ever think of this?! With an incredible knack for taking everyday items and creating extraordinary party food, Norene is now sharing her step-by-step instructions in her fabulous second book. For years, I have hoped Norene would share her creative talents with us—how exciting to have her instruc-tions all together in one book! You will see how easy it can be to make the cutest treats you have ever seen. Organized instructions make it easy for you to delight your family, your friends, and yourself . . . and to turn your next party into a Sweet Treat for everyone!"
—*Lydia Menzies, party stylist and blogger at* The Party Wagon

"*Party with Sweet Treats* is terrific! The incredibly creative Norene Cox has done it again with lots more fun, easy ways to treat the children. This is sure to make any party truly magical."
—*Victoria Threader, owner of* Victorious Cupcakes (UK)

party
with
Sweet
Treats

Front Table Books
An imprint of Cedar Fort, Inc.
Springville, Utah

Norene Cox

dressed-up goodies
for EVERY occasion

MONOPOLY & TWISTER ® & © 2014 Hasbro, Inc.
Used with permission.

ISBN 13: 978-1-4621-1602-7

Published by Front Table Books, an imprint of Cedar Fort, Inc.
2373 W. 700 S., Springville, UT 84663
Distributed by Cedar Fort, Inc., www.cedarfort.com

Library of Congress Control Number: 2014956161

Cover design by Bekah Claussen and Lauren Error
Cover design © 2015 Lyle Mortimer
Edited by Justin Greer

Printed in the United States of America

10 9 8 7 6 5 4 3 2 1

For my sweet sons, Austin & Carson.
You give me reason to celebrate each and every day.

Contents

Introduction

I have been told that I have a Willy Wonka way at looking at things. I suppose that is true, because when I walk down the candy aisle at a grocery or drug store, I don't really see candy. I see all of the possibilities that I can make out of gumdrops and taffy, like frogs and dogs or hats and cats. Crafting with food is so much fun; it's something I learned to do when my boys were in elementary school and I was their room mom.

I found that the kids thought decorating treats was the best part of their classroom parties. Using store-bought cookies, candy, and cakes, the possibilities were endless! I wholeheartedly agree that it was much more fun creating sweet treats than waiting for cakes to bake or cookies to cool—getting right down to the decorating is where it was at!

When I first started my website, partypinching.com, I quickly came to realize that my treats were so popular because people liked the idea that "homemade" didn't have to mean "made from scratch." It has been so heartwarming to receive photos of my treats being re-created by families, kids in classrooms, church groups, and senior centers! I especially love hearing about new holiday traditions that include making my edible crafts!

Party with Sweet Treats is the perfect complement to my first book, *Sweet Treats for the Holidays*, which features fun treats from Halloween through New Year's. There are so many reasons to celebrate; I just had to create more fun, edible crafts that you can enjoy all year long!

Whether it's Bunny Marshmallow Pops for Easter, Twinkie Toes for a baby shower, or Peanut Butter Checkers for game night, you'll love to make these simple and sweet adorable snacks!

Let's face it, decorating the treats is the best part, and here I show you how using store-bought cookies and snack cakes.

So grab some candy, cookies, and a can of frosting, and let's get this party started!

Tips & Tricks

Here are a few basic tips and tricks for making your candy creations even cuter.

Make your own recipe for fun

The main ingredient for making cute food is FUN! Your imagination is your best tool for creating adorable desserts. Feel free to make substitutions for candy and such. Use M&M's instead of jelly beans, Life Savers candies in the place of mints, brownies rather than Rice Krispie Treats, or homemade cookies instead of store-bought. Don't be afraid to put your own personal spin on these sweet treats.

Create an imagination station

Before starting, make sure you have all of your ingredients and tools handy. If the kids are helping, then have small, personal portions of candy and sprinkles for each child.

Stock your pantry

Keep these staples on hand so you can make edible crafts at a moment's notice!

Sprinkles

I admit that I have something of a sprinkle obsession. I collect sprinkles in all shapes and sizes, all colors and textures, for all holidays and occasions. Racks and stacks of them. But here is a rundown of the most common sprinkles.

• Pearls: small round balls of sugar, but be careful—these can be hard on your teeth!
• Jumbo shapes: extra-large flat sprinkles with circle, tree, heart, and flower shapes, just to name a few.
• Mini chip crunch: tiny candy-coated chocolate chips in multiple colors.
• Nonpareils: super tiny balls that like to bounce all over your kitchen counter.
• Small shapes: these sprinkles are sometimes called *quins* and come in all different shapes and holiday themes.
• Sugar sprinkles (or sanding sugar): these sprinkles are probably the most common and resemble fine sugar. They come in all colors of the rainbow.

- Sugar crystals: sugar sprinkles that have a large grain and a coarse texture.
- Mini shapes: these sprinkles are like the small shapes, but tiny and adorable.
- Confetti: flat, round discs in black, white, pastel, or primary colors.
- Dragées: small round balls of sugar coated with a metallic finish.
- Jimmies: long skinny sprinkles often used on top of ice cream!

Candy Coating
The 2 main types of candy coating I like to use are the bags of wafer candy melts and the bark-type candy coating (such as CandiQuik).

Candy
Crafting with candy is the best part of making cute food. There are so many bright colors, shapes, sizes, yummy flavors, and textures that you can let your imagination run wild! Grocery stores, gas stations, convenience stores, and party stores all have an assortment of candies that will spark your creativity. I love to go to grocery stores that sell candy in bulk bins so I can pick and choose how many I want and the colors I need!

Food Coloring
- Liquid dye: Available at your local grocery store, this dye gives a soft, muted tint to your frosting or coconut.
- Gel paste: Found at craft and specialty stores and on-line, a little (and I really mean a little—like a toothpick full) goes a long way for rich, vibrant colors.
- Food color mist: A great way to add color to frosting, cookies, and cereal, and let's face it, sometimes it's just super fun to pretend you are a graffiti artist.

Cookies
Transform store-bought cookies into super cute treats. Look at them as a blank canvas to embellish upon and turn ordinary cookies into extraordinary ones!

More Sweet Stuff
Graham crackers, Rice Krispie Treat bars, marshmallows, cupcakes, snack cakes and mini donuts are just a few store-bought supplies to make life easier.

Resources and Suppliers

If you have difficulty finding items listed in the recipes at your local grocery or craft stores, here are some online resources and suppliers.

Edible markers
>   Americolor: www.americolorcorp.com

Candy coating
>   CandiQuik: www.candiquik.com
>   Make'n Mold: www.makenmold.com
>   Wilton: www.wilton.com

Specialty and seasonal candy
>   Candy.com: www.candy.com
>   Candy Warehouse: www.candywarehouse.com
>   SweetWorks: www.sweetworks.net
>   Sixlets Candies

Candy eyes
>   Wilton: www.wilton.com

Chocolate truffles
>   Lindt: www.lindtusa.com

Food coloring mist:
>   Wilton: www.wilton.com

Sprinkles
>   Global Sugar Art: www.globalsugarart.com
>   Shop Bakers Nook: www.shopbakersnook.com
>   Wilton: www.wilton.com

Craft stores
Regional craft stores usually carry a variety of supplies, sprinkles, food coloring mist, candy eyes, candy coating, food coloring, and so on.
>   Hobby Lobby: www.hobbylobby.com
>   Jo-Ann Fabric and Craft Stores: www.joann.com
>   Michaels - www.michaels.com

Tools

These are my must-have tools. They can be found at any grocery or craft store, but you probably already have most of them!

- Kitchen shears
- Toothpicks
- Small knife
- Edible markers
- Parchment or wax paper
- Paper straws
- Popsicle sticks
- Paper drink umbrellas
- Fondant roller
- Cookie cutters
- Lollipop sticks

BUDGET FRIENDLY PARTY IDEAS
CUTE FOOD INSPIRATON

Party Pinching Tips

One of the reasons I started my website partypinching.com was to provide budget-friendly party ideas. Fun parties and great ideas don't have to break the bank; with imagination and a sincere effort to make an event special, the personal touches will, I believe, make your guests sense the love and thoughtfulness in all that you have created for the occasion.

Details are what impress your guests the most. They will be amazed and appreciative of the thoughtfulness and the creativity your party possesses—and they won't believe you did it all on a budget.

Dessert tables

Dessert tables are a great way to show off your sweet treats! A great staple to have for any dessert theme is a white tablecloth. More budget-friendly tablecloths are burlap, butcher paper, a pretty quilt, and fabric by the yard. Backdrops are fun, and a money-saving idea is to create them with fabric, balloons, ribbons, or streamers!

White plates, cake stands, and platters

Inexpensive plates and platters can be found at your local thrift shops, party stores, craft stores, and dollar stores. These white plates are the perfect canvas to show off your works of art! Plastic ones are easy on the budget and can be used over and over again. Inexpensive cake plates can be made with a candleholder with a plate on top. Appetizer dishes and glasses are so cute that you can put just about anything in them and it would be adorable. Put popsicles in small parfait glasses, candy in itty bitty cups, and lemonade in martini glasses. They even make inexpensive plastic ones that you can find online or discount party stores.

End of the season sales

A great way to save money is to pick up seasonal items after the holiday is over. You can get great bargains on sprinkles, decorations, cupcake liners, and more!

Gotta have it

If you find something that you LOVE and it would be the perfect centerpiece or decoration for your party, it's okay, buy it. One pricey element to build the rest of your budget-friendly party around is a great way to fool your friends into thinking you spent a fortune when you really didn't. Great finds can always be found at stores like HomeGoods, Pier One, World Market, and Target.

Invites

I know that e-vites are convenient, but there is nothing like receiving a good old-fashioned invitation in the mail. Whether you make them yourself or purchase them, don't forget that this is a great way to set the mood for your party. And please don't forget the kids—my boys were so excited about invitations when they were little that they would put them under their pillows and sleep with them.

Goody bags

No matter what their age, your guests will love a goody bag to take home. Fill small cellophane bags with a cute Bunny Marshmallow Pop for Easter, or a Balloon Oreo for a birthday, and tie with a pretty ribbon. Just one more detail to make your guests feel special.

For more budget-friendly party, dessert table, & cute food ideas, please visit my website www.partypinching.com

Tutorials

Candy Coating Cookies

Coating cookies in candy using either wafers or bark is easy if you follow these simple steps.

1. Melt your candy coating in a microwave according to package instructions.
2. Pour the coating in a deep container and dip the cookie in the melted coating until completely submerged.
3. Lift out with fork and tap against the container to remove excess coating.
4. Carefully slide the coated cookie onto parchment paper to set.

Decorating with Frosting

Piping frosting on a cupcake or cookie using a decorating tip is easier than you think.

1. Place decorating tip in a disposable pastry bag. Place bag in a tall glass and fold edges over so it is easy to fill. Spoon frosting into bag.
2. Twist the end of the bag so the frosting doesn't ooze out when you squeeze it.
3. For a classic swirl, hold your bag over the cupcake with the tip at approximately ½ inch above the cupcake at a 90-degree angle.
4. Gently squeeze the bag with even pressure starting from the outside of the cupcake, making a clockwise motion and working your way inside the cupcake.
5. When you reach the middle, stop squeezing and lift up.

I use 3 kinds of decorating tips in this book:
1M Open Star tip from Wilton
4B Open Star tip from Wilton (like a French tip)
233 Grass/Fur tip from Wilton

No-Bake Cake Pops

Ingredients
snack cakes (I use Little Debbie Fancy Cakes or Zebra Cakes—they have the perfect cake-to-frosting ratio for cake pops. 1 snack cake = 1 cake pop)
1 (12-oz.) bag candy coating wafers
lollipop sticks

1. Unwrap snack cakes (there are 2 in a package) and mush in a bowl.
2. Roll mushed cake into balls.
3. Melt candy coating according to package instructions. Dip end of lollipop sticks in candy melts and push halfway through pop. Freeze for 1 hour.
4. Dip cake pop into melted candy coating. Once covered, pull up and gently tap the stick on the side of the bowl to remove excess candy coating. Place stick into Styrofoam block to dry.

That's it. Three ingredients. Mush, roll, freeze, dip, done. Booyah.

Holidays

Chinese New Year

chinese rice krispie treat dragons

Sweet dragons to bring good fortune to your Chinese New Year festivities!
Lucky little dragons made from Rice Krispie Treats and fruit snacks.

2 store-bought Rice Krispie Treat bars
4 red Fruit by the Foot
1 (16-oz.) can vanilla frosting
8 red Jujube candies
8 candy eyes
8 mini red M&M's
1 yellow Fruit Roll-up

Makes **4** chinese rice krispie treat dragons

1. Cut Rice Krispie Treat bars into 1 × 1¾ inch rectangles.

2. Wrap the red Fruit by the Foot around the edge of a rectangle. Trim to fit. The Fruit by the Foot should stick to itself, or you can secure with a little frosting.

3. Cut a small piece of red Fruit by the Foot to fit the top of the Rice Krispie Treat. Attach with frosting.

4. With a toothpick dipped in frosting, attach 2 red Jujube candies at one end of the Rice Krispie Treat for ears.

5. Attach 2 candy eyes and 2 mini M&M's for the nose with frosting.

6. Cut 3 small triangles out of the yellow Fruit Roll-up. With a toothpick dipped in frosting, attach one triangle in the middle of the eyes and one triangle on each side of the head.

7. Make the tail using the remaining red Fruit by the Foot, and pinch it to make it wavy so it looks like ribbon.

8. Attach to head; it should stick by itself, or you may use frosting to secure.

panda snack cakes

Perfectly pandalicious.
Create your own soft, sweet pandas from coconut marshmallow snack cakes. Everyone will be bamboozled over how unbearably cute these are!

**approximately ¹/₂ cup white candy
    coating wafers**
2 white Hostess Sno Ball snack cakes
4 Mini Oreos
1 Tootsie Roll
4 white pearl sprinkles
2 dark brown Mini M&M's

Makes **2** *panda snack cakes*

1. Melt white candy coating according to package instructions.

2. Using a knife, make 2 small cuts in the top of the Sno Ball for the ears to fit in. Dip the lower half of the Mini Oreos into the melted candy coating and place into the slits on top of the Sno Ball for the ears.

3. Soften the Tootsie Roll in the microwave for approximately 5 seconds.

4. Break off 2 small pieces of the Tootsie Roll and use your fingers to make them into flat, oval shapes approximately ½-inch long.

5. Attach the Tootsie Roll ovals to the front of the Sno Ball for eyes, using the melted white candy coating.

6. Using a toothpick dipped in melted candy coating, attach the pearl sprinkles in the center of the flattened Tootsie Rolls.

7. Attach the dark brown Mini M&M to the front of the Sno Ball for the nose using a toothpick dipped in the melted candy coating.

Valentine's Day

sweetheart mice

Cute little critters that will steal your heart!
Treat your sweetie to this funny little valentine!

2 white Jordan almonds
Approximately ¹/₂ cup white candy
 coating wafers
4 white Smarties candies
2 mini pink confetti sprinkles
black edible marker
1 miniature peanut butter cup
1 Rolo candy
1 large red heart sprinkle
2 small white heart sprinkles
2 white chocolate peanut butter cups
red, pink, and white small heart sprinkles

Makes **2** *sweetheart mice*

1. Melt white candy coating according to package instructions.

2. Using the melted candy coating, attach 2 white Smarties candies to the top of a white Jordan almond for ears. Hold in place until set.

3. With a toothpick dipped in the white melted candy coating, attach the mini pink confetti sprinkle to the end of the white Jordan almond for the nose.

4. Make 2 dots for eyes on the white Jordan almond with the black edible marker.

5. For the girl mouse, attach the head to an upside down miniature peanut butter cup. For the boy mouse, attach the head to an upside down Rolo candy.

6. Using a toothpick dipped in the white melted candy coating, attach the large heart sprinkle to the middle of the miniature peanut butter cup and the 2 small white heart sprinkles pointing towards each other to the Rolo candy for the bow tie.

7. Attach the heads to the miniature peanut butter cup and the Rolo candy with melted candy coating.

8. Secure the mice to the white peanut butter cup with melted candy coating.

9. With a toothpick dipped in melted candy coating, draw a rim around the edge of the white peanut butter cup. Immediately arrange red, pink, and white heart sprinkles on top. Let dry completely.

love bug cookies

Lovely little lady bugs to sweeten up your day!
You'll have a sweet spot in your heart for these adorable chocolate marshmallow cookies!

1 (12-oz.) bag red candy coating wafers
12 chocolate-coated marshmallow
         cookies (such as Mallomars)
24 candy eyes
pink heart sprinkles
black round confetti sprinkles
black edible marker

Makes 12 love bug cookies

1. Melt red candy coating according to package instructions.

2. Dip half of a chocolate-coated marshmallow cookie into the red candy coating. Place on wax or parchment paper.

3. Arrange pink heart sprinkles and black round confetti sprinkles on the red candy coating while still wet.

4. With a toothpick dipped in melted candy coating, attach eyes to the top of the cookie.

5. Let dry completely.

6. Using a black edible marker, draw a line down the middle of the red candy-coated half of the cookie.

perfect pair cookie

You are the sweet to my treat!
Create cookies that complement each other! We go together like mac & cheese, bubble & gum, shake & bake! The possibilities are endless!

1 heart-shaped sugar cookie, homemade or store-bought
1 (7-oz.) pouch pink cookie icing
red and white pearl candies
1 vanilla Tootsie Roll
1 orange Tootsie Roll
red heart sprinkles
black edible marker

> Makes **1** perfect pair cookie

For the cookie:

1. Using cookie icing pouch, frost the top of a heart cookie.

2. Arrange candy pearls around the edge of the heart cookie, alternating red and white.

For the macaroni:

1. Microwave a vanilla Tootsie Roll for about 7 seconds so it can be easily shaped.

2. Using about half of the Tootsie Roll, form into a macaroni shape.

3. With a toothpick, make a hole in each end of the macaroni.

4. Draw a smiley face with a black edible marker.

For the Cheese:

1. Microwave an orange Tootsie Roll for about 7 seconds so it can be easily shaped.

2. Form into a small triangle so it resembles cheese.

3. Using a very small frosting piping tip, make holes in the cheese.

4. Draw a smiley face with a black edible marker.

5. Place 2 red heart sprinkles in the middle of the cookie.

Tip: Let your imagination run wild with these cookies! Using various candies like Starburst, Tootsie Rolls, and Airheads, along with assorted sprinkles, you can make so many cute combos!

You are the ...

EGG TO MY BACON

BUBBLE TO MY GUM

BREAD TO MY BUTTER

SHAKE TO MY BAKE

GLAZE TO MY DONUT

MILK TO MY COOKIE

PEANUT TO MY BUTTER

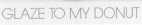

STRAW TO MY BERRY

LOVE OF MY LIFE

puppy love cookies

Doggone delicious.
Candy coat some Oreos for pawsitively perfect puppy cookies that will have everyone begging for more.

1 (12-oz.) bag white candy coating wafers
12 Oreo cookies
12 Cherry flavored (red) Tootsie Rolls
12 pink Necco wafers
12 mini black jelly beans
12 jumbo red heart sprinkles
black edible marker

Makes **12** *puppy love cookies*

1. Melt white candy coating wafers according to package instructions.

2. Place Oreo cookie on fork and submerge cookie into the melted candy coating, covering it thoroughly.

3. Lift cookie out of the candy coating and tap fork lightly against bowl to remove excess coating.

4. Place on wax or parchment paper.

5. Soften red Tootsie Roll in microwave for approximately 7 seconds.

6. Cut Tootsie Roll in half and use your fingers to make each half into a teardrop shape. Flatten.

7. Press to the side of the cookie for the ears.

8. Place pink Necco wafer on top of cookie.

9. Using a toothpick dipped in candy coating, attach the jelly bean to the top of the pink Necco wafer for the nose.

10. Place a red jumbo heart sprinkle just to the upper right of the Necco wafer on top of the cookie.

11. Let dry completely.

12. Draw mouth on the pink Necco wafer using the black edible marker. Add one dot on top of the red jumbo heart sprinkle and another dot on the other side on the white cookie for the eyes.

Tip: For step-by step instructions on how to dip Oreos, see page xvi.

brownie love bites

Delightful desserts for your Valentine.
Simply elegant, these tasty treats will make your sweetheart think you've been baking all day, but you'll fall in LOVE with how easy these are to assemble!

24 store-bought brownie bites
1 (16-oz.) can of milk chocolate frosting
24 fresh red raspberries
large Open Star (Wilton 1M) decorating tip with piping bag (optional)

1. Frost the top of the brownie with chocolate frosting.

2. Place fresh raspberry on top of frosting in the middle.

That's it. I promise. You're welcome.

Tip: For step-by-step instructions on how to pipe frosting, see page xvi.

Makes **24** *brownie love bites*

St. Patrick's Day

pot of gold oreo pops

Your little leprechauns will love this magical treat!
Celebrate St. Patrick's Day with these yummy cookie pops!

24 Oreo Fudge Cremes (I used the mint-flavored ones)
1 (16-oz.) can of chocolate frosting
12 lollipop sticks
6 rainbow sour belt candies
36 green Mini M&M's
12 green jimmie sprinkles
36 yellow M&M's

Makes **12** *pot of gold oreo pops*

1. Spread the bottom of 1 Oreo Fudge Creme with frosting. Place one end of the lollipop stick in the middle of the frosting.

2. Spread frosting on the bottom of another Oreo Fudge Creme and place the frosting side down on top of the other frosted Oreo Fudge Creme so the lollipop stick is sandwiched in between.

3. Using a sharp knife and in one motion, chop off the top part of the cookies to resemble a pot.

4. Cut the rainbow sour belts in half. Attach each end to the top of the cookie using frosting so it forms a rainbow.

5. Using a toothpick dipped in frosting, attach the 3 green Mini M&M's and the green jimmie sprinkle to the front of the cookie pop to resemble a clover.

6. Attach the 3 yellow M&M's to the sliced part of the cookies under the rainbow with frosting for the gold coins.

Tip: If the frosting isn't holding the rainbow or you would like the candy to set up faster on the cookie pop, substitute melted chocolate for the frosting.

little leprechaun cupcakes

Wee leprechaun cookies to top your cupcakes!
Lucky little cupcakes that your kiddos will have fun creating!

**approximately ¹/₂ cup yellow candy
coating wafers
12 green gumdrops
2 green apple sour straws
12 vanilla wafer cookies
84 orange Mini M&M's
black edible marker
12 frosted cupcakes**

Makes **12** little
leprechaun cupcakes

1. Melt candy coating according to package instructions.

2. Dip the bottom of a green gumdrop in the yellow melted candy coating.

3. Cut the green apple sour straws into approximately 1-inch pieces.

4. Place green gumdrop on top of a 1-inch piece of sour straw for hat. Let dry.

5. Using a toothpick dipped in yellow melted candy coating, attach 7 orange Mini M&M's to the bottom rim of the vanilla wafer.

6. Attach gumdrop hat to the top of the cookie with melted candy coating.

7. Draw smiley face using a black edible marker on the vanilla wafer cookie. Place cookie on top of the frosted cupcake.

mini shamrock cakes

Cute clover cakes for St. Paddy's Day.
Lads and lasses alike will love these magical mini shamrock treats!

1 (16-oz.) frozen pound cake
    (such as Sara Lee)
mini shamrock cookie cutter
1 (16-oz.) can white frosting
green sugar sprinkles

1. Cut pound cake in approximately ¾-inch slices.

2. Use the mini cookie cutter to cut shamrock shapes out of the pound cake.

3. Lightly frost the tops of the shamrocks.

4. Pour the sugar sprinkles onto a shallow plate.

5. Dip the frosted top of the shamrock into the sugar sprinkles.

Makes approximately **24** *mini shamrock cakes*

pretty peep cake

It's Peeptastic.
A sweet little cake that is unbelievably easy to decorate! Perfect for your Easter brunch!

6- or 8-inch round cake
1 (16-oz.) can of white frosting
Necco wafers (approximately 4 rolls)
2 pink bunny Peeps
1 purple bunny Peep
2 Wilton Icing Flowers (pink)
2 green heart sprinkles
1 yellow confetti sprinkle
1 white jumbo flower sprinkle
1 small yellow flower sprinkle
1 mini paper cupcake liner
1 yellow paper drink umbrella
2 toothpicks

Makes **1** *pretty peep cake*

1. Frost cake using white frosting.

2. Press the Necco wafers into the frosting on the side of the cake, starting on the bottom row first, alternating colors.

3. Cut one pink Peep in half with kitchen shears.

4. Poke a toothpick in the middle of a mini cupcake liner.

5. Push bunny Peep head into the top of the toothpick and press on the bottom of the cupcake liner so it looks like a skirt. With frosting, attach flower sprinkles to the bottom of one ear.

6. Using kitchen shears, cut a purple Peep bunny and a pink Peep bunny in half.

7. Attach pink head to purple body with frosting. Add heart and round confetti sprinkles for the bow tie using frosting. Press a toothpick in the bottom of the bunny.

8. Place Peeps and umbrella on top of cake.

sweet bunny truffles

Simply "EAR"resistible.
Hop to it! Yummy cottontail cuties that will be the hit of your Easter celebration!

Approximately ¹/₄ cup white candy coating wafers
12 pink candy buttons
12 white chocolate truffles (such as Lindt)
48 almond slices
pink edible marker
black edible marker
12 snowflake sprinkles

Makes **12** *sweet bunny truffles*

1. Melt candy coating according to package instructions.

2. Using a toothpick dipped in melted white candy coating, attach the pink candy button to the front of the white chocolate truffle.

3. Color in the middle of 2 of the almond slices with a pink edible marker for the ears. Dip the bottom of the almond slices in the melted white candy coating and attach to the top of the truffle. You will have to hold these in place until set.

4. Using a black edible marker, make 2 dots right above the nose for eyes.

5. Draw 3 lines on the edge of 2 almond slices for the feet with a black edible marker. Attach to the bottom of the truffle with melted candy coating.

6. Attach a snowflake sprinkle to the other side of the truffle for the tail with melted white chocolate.

Tip: These pudgy little bunnies make great cupcake toppers too!

chicks on a stick

Egg-sploding with cuteness.
Get crackin' and make these fun Chicks on a Stick from candy coated almonds and white chocolate Kit Kat bars!

**Approximately ¹/₂ cup white candy
      coating wafers
8 yellow Jordan almonds
8 orange mini chip sprinkles
black edible marker
1 white chocolate Kit Kat bar
¹/₄ cup shredded sweetened coconut
green food coloring
flower sprinkles**

Makes **8** *chicks on a stick*

1. Melt white candy coating according to package instructions.

2. Using a toothpick dipped in melted candy coating, attach an orange mini chip to the front of the yellow Jordan almond.

3. Make 2 dots with the black edible marker on the Jordan almond for eyes.

4. Break apart the Kit Kat bar. Attach the chick to the bottom of one Kit Kat stick using melted candy coating. Hold into place until set.

5. Put the coconut in a plastic zipper bag. Place 1 drop of green food coloring in the bag and shake. Add more food coloring, one drop at a time, to get the desired green color.

6. Spread a thin layer of melted candy coating on the Kit Kat stick. Immediately press on green coconut.

7. With a toothpick dipped in melted candy coating, attach flower sprinkles on top of the green coconut.

peanut butter cup easter baskets

Make these for somebunny special.
It's safe to put all of your eggs into one basket when you decide to make this yummy peanut butter dessert!

1 (16-oz.) can of white frosting
green food coloring
12 white peanut butter cups
6 green apple sour straws
36 mini jelly beans

Makes **12** easter baskets

1. Mix a few drops of green food coloring into the can of white frosting until you get the desired color.

2. Using a grass icing tip, pipe the green frosting onto the top of the peanut butter cup to make it look like grass, or just frost the middle of the peanut butter cup with a knife.

3. Cut the green apple sour straws in half. Gently press the ends of the sour straw into the peanut butter cup for the handle.

4. Place 3 jelly beans in the middle of the grass frosting.

Tip: It may be easier to poke small holes in the peanut butter cup with a toothpick or wooden skewer first and then press in the sour straw ends.

mini bunny brownie garden

*Lettuce make some goodies for the Easter Bunny to show that we carrot about him.
We leave cookies for Santa, why not some sweets for the Easter Bunny? Super cute garden goodies made from store-bought brownies!*

**9 little brownie bites
(such as Entenmann's)**
1 (16-oz.) can of chocolate frosting
3 Oreos
1/2 cup green candy coating wafers
9 Mike and Ike candy (orange)
9 clover-shaped sprinkles
**approximately 1/2 cup Frosted Flakes or
Corn Flakes cereal**
**1 (1.5-oz.) can green food color spray
mist**
pink Wilton Icing Flowers

Makes **1** *mini bunny brownie garden*

For the ground

1. Frost top of brownie.

2. Put Oreo cookies in a plastic zipper bag. Using a rolling pin, finely crush the cookies.

3. Place Oreo crumbs on top of frosted brownie.

For the carrots

1. Melt green candy coating according to package instructions.

2. Using a toothpick dipped in the melted candy coating, place a small amount of the candy melts onto the bottom end of the orange Mike and Ike candy.

3. Place the shamrock sprinkle stem side down on top of the coating and hold in place until set.

4. Put 3 carrots on top of brownie.

For the lettuce

1. Spread Frosted Flakes on parchment paper or foil. Spray with green food color mist. Let dry and turn over and spray again.

2. Arrange about 10 flakes on top of brownie so it resembles lettuce.

For the flowers

1. Place the store-bought pink Wilton Icing Flower on top of the brownie.

bunny marshmallow pops

Everybunny will love these.
Your guests will be all ears when they hear that you've made Easter Bunny Marshmallow Pops!

12 regular size marshmallows
12 lollipop sticks
24 white Jordan almonds
pink edible marker
¹/₂ cup white candy coating wafers
black edible marker
12 small pink jelly beans

Makes **12** bunny marshmallow pops

1. Push lollipop stick in the bottom of the marshmallow.

2. Using the pink edible marker, color the middle of the white Jordan almonds so they look like bunny ears.

3. Melt white candy coating according to package instructions.

4. Dip the narrow end of 2 of the Jordan almonds into the melted candy coating and place on top of the marshmallow for the ears. Hold into place until set.

5. With a toothpick dipped in white melted candy coating, attach a mini pink jelly bean to the middle of the marshmallow for the nose. Hold into place until set.

6. Make 2 dots on the marshmallow with the black edible marker for the eyes.

April Fools' Day

chicken pretenders

Fake & Bake.
Actually, there is no need to bake these chicken tenders! Made from Rice Krispie Treats and crushed Corn Flakes, these mock bocks are sure to fool your family!

3 store-bought Rice Krispie Treat bars
1/2 cup finely crushed Corn Flake cereal

Makes **3** chicken pretenders

1. Flatten a Rice Krispie Treat bar and shape to resemble a chicken tender with your hands.

2. Pour the finely crushed Corn Flake cereal on a shallow plate.

3. Press the treat into the crushed Corn Flakes. Flip over and press to coat the other side.

Tip: Spoon lemon yogurt into a small dish to resemble honey mustard sauce.

buf-"faux"-lo wings

Fool your friends and family with these sweet treats!
These buffalo wings actually fooled my son. He saw them on the kitchen counter after school, bit into one, and said, "Hey—what?" Then he said "Mmmm" and took the entire plate with him to watch TV.

6 store-bought Rice Krispie Treat bars
1 Tbsp. orange juice
1 cup dark brown sugar
4 pieces of green licorice
1/4 cup marshmallow creme
**   (Marshmallow Fluff)**
3 mini marshmallows

Makes **6** buf-"faux"-lo wings

1. Shape Rice Krispie Treats to look like chicken wings.

2. Mix 1 cup dark brown sugar and 1 tablespoon orange juice. The mixture will be very thick.

3. Generously coat the wings by brushing on the mixture. Let dry on parchment paper.

4. Cut the green licorice in half to look like celery.

5. Chop up some mini marshmallows and mix in the marshmallow creme for the blue cheese dipping sauce. Put in small bowl on the side.

Tip: If you want them to have the red buffalo sauce look, you may add a little red food coloring to the brown sugar coating.

chili? not really.

Bean there. Done that.
They'll love this April Fools' Day prank. Because really, who is ever disappointed with chocolate cake? Perfect for Super Bowl parties too!

4 chocolate snack cakes
1 (16-oz.) can chocolate frosting
20 red or brown jelly beans (or Boston baked beans - the candy coated peanuts)
¹/₄ cup sweetened shredded coconut
orange food coloring

Makes **4** chili? not really. bowls

1. Cut up the snack cakes to fit a small bowl. You may need a different number of snack cakes depending on the size of your bowl.

2. Spread a layer of chocolate frosting evenly over the snack cakes.

3. Place jelly beans in the frosting.

4. Put the coconut in a plastic zipper bag, add a drop of orange food coloring, and shake. You may add more food coloring one drop at a time to get the desired "cheese" color.

5. Sprinkle the orange coconut in the middle of the bowl.

Tip: For an easier version, substitute store-bought chocolate pudding for the snack cakes and frosting.

shepherd's pie! you lie!

A deceiving dinner to serve on April Fools' Day.
Chocolate Rice Krispie Treat Bars topped with marshmallow creme make a creative counterfeit casserole!

small casserole dish
4 Rice Krispie Treat Double Chocolate
    Chunk Bars
3 green lime flavored Tootsie Rolls
3 orange flavored Tootsie Rolls
1 (7-oz.) jar of marshmallow creme (or
Marshmallow Fluff)

Makes **1** *shepherd's pie! you lie!*
casserole

1. Press the Rice Krispie Treat chocolate bars into a small casserole dish to form a nice layer. You may need a different number of bars depending on the size of your dish.

2. Soften the Tootsie Rolls in the microwave for approximately 7 seconds.

3. Using the softened green Tootsie Rolls, break off small pieces and roll them into small pea shapes.

4. Using the softened orange Tootsie Rolls, break off small pieces and shape them into little diced carrots.

5. Press the peas and carrots on top of the chocolate Rice Krispie Treat bars in the dish.

6. Spread a thick layer of marshmallow creme over the treats.

7. Put under the broiler in the oven for a few seconds to brown the top, if desired.

"not"-zarella sticks

It ain't easy being cheesy.
These cereal-coated cakes dipped in strawberry "marinara" sauce really do make a great dessert. No foolin'.

1 (10.75-oz.) frozen pound cake (such as Sara Lee)
1 (16-oz.) can white frosting
1/2 cup finely crushed Corn Flakes cereal
green sugar sprinkles

Makes **12** "not" - zarella sticks

1. Slice pound cake in half.

2. Trim off crust and cut into 1-inch sticks lengthwise.

3. Spread frosting on all sides of the sticks.

4. Pour the finely crushed Corn Flakes on a shallow plate.

5. Roll the frosted sticks in the crushed Corn Flakes until completely coated.

6. Sprinkle the green sugar sprinkles on top to resemble Italian spices.

Tip: Place strawberry jam in a small dish for "marinara" dipping sauce.

Mother's Day

teacup toppers

Here's a sweet opportunitea to impress your mom!
Brew up some mini meringue cookie cup toppers to show off your creativitea!

12 store-bought small meringue cookies
¹/₂ cup white candy coating wafers
12 pink flower sprinkles
pink mini flower sprinkles
12 white candy coating wafers
1 white Airhead candy or white fondant
brown edible marker
12 frosted cupcakes

Makes **12** teacup toppers

1. Slice the point off of the top of the meringue cookie.

2. Melt white candy coating according to package instructions.

3. Turn a white candy coating wafer, so the flat side is up.

4. Dip the sliced end of the cookie into the melted candy coating and attach to the flat side of a white candy coating wafer so they resemble a cup and saucer.

5. Using a toothpick dipped in white melted candy coating, attach the pink flower sprinkle on the front in the middle of the meringue cookie teacup.

6. Attach the pink mini flower sprinkles with a toothpick dipped in white melted candy coating round the edge of the white candy coating wafer saucer.

7. Break off a small piece of the white Airhead candy and roll into a rope. Curve into a handle and attach to the meringue cookie with the melted white candy coating.

8. Color in the top of the cookie with a brown edible marker to resemble tea.

9. Place the teacup on top of the frosted cupcake.

purse cookies

Mom will love to get her clutches on these cookies.
Get purse-sonal and create your mom a treat that will make her Prada of you.

**12 store-bought sugar or shortbread
    cookies
1 (16-oz.) can of white frosting
red food coloring
¹/₂ cup white candy coating wafers
12 vanilla Tootsie Rolls
white pearl candy**

Makes **12** purse cookies

1. Place 1 or 2 drops of red food coloring in the can of white frosting. Stir to incorporate so the frosting turns a light pink color.

2. Using a Wilton M1 piping tip and icing bag, pipe a swirl of frosting on top of a cookie or simply spread the frosting on top of the cookie with a knife. Let dry completely until frosting is hard.

3. Cut cookie in half.

4. Melt candy coating according to package instructions.

5. Spread the melted candy coating on the unfrosted side of the cookie halves.

6. Attach the cookie halves together with the melted candy coating side.

7. Place cookie on plate cut side down.

8. Soften Tootsie Rolls in microwave for approximately 7 seconds.

9. Roll a Tootsie Roll into a "U" shape for the purse handle.

10. Attach the white pearl candy to the Tootsie Roll handle with melted candy coating. Let dry completely.

11. Dip each end of the Tootsie Roll handle into the melted candy coating and attach to the top of the cookie.

Tip: For step-by-step instructions on how to pipe frosting, see page xvi.

Father's Day

candy bar television remote

A chocolate bar so awesome it'll make Dad lose control.
No treat will come remotely close to a chocolate version of your father's favorite toy.

1 chocolate candy bar
1/2 cup chocolate candy coating wafers
1 red M&M
1 blue M&M
9 dark brown M&M's
Mini M&M's
White Tic Tac mints

1. Melt chocolate candy coating according to package instructions.

2. Flip over the chocolate candy bar and use a toothpick dipped in the melted candy coating to attach the various candies in a pattern that resembles a remote control.

Makes **1** candy bar remote

brownie grill bites

So barbecute.
A perfect goody for the grillmaster.

6 little brownie bites (such as Entenmann's)
1 (.67-oz.) tube of black writing gel
12 red Mike and Ike candies
2 green Mike and Ike candies
2 yellow Mike and Ike candies
2 pink Mike and Ike candies
6 toothpicks
18 lollipop sticks
$1/2$ cup chocolate melted candy coating
12 dark brown M&M's

*Makes **6** brownie grill bites*

1. With the black writing gel, make a circle around the top edge of the brownie bite. Then, make grill lines with the writing gel inside of the circle.

2. Using the black edible marker, make little grill marks on the red Mike and Ike candies so they look like hot dogs. Place hot dogs on top of brownie grill.

3. Slice the green, yellow, orange, and pink Mike and Ike candies into thirds.

4. Place one sliced Mike and Ike of each color onto a toothpick for the skewer. Place on brownie grill.

5. Cut lollipop sticks into approximately 2-inch lengths. Push 2 sticks into the bottom of the brownie.

6. Melt chocolate candy coating wafers according to package instructions.

7. Attach the M&M's to the bottom of the lollipop sticks for wheels using the melted candy coating.

4th of July

red, white, and blue watermelon cookies

A sweet slice of the 4th of July.
A proud little cookie that's one in a melon!

12 store-bought sugar cookies
1 (16-oz.) can white frosting
red sugar sprinkles
blue sugar sprinkles
white star sprinkles

Makes **24** red, white, and blue watermelon cookies

1. Spread frosting on top of the sugar cookie.

2. With your fingers, very carefully sprinkle the edge of the frosting circle with blue sugar sprinkles.

3. Make a circle in the center of the cookie with red sugar sprinkles, leaving a white ring of frosting between the red inner circle and the blue rim.

4. Press the white star sprinkles in a circle in the red sprinkled part.

5. Cut cookie in half.

uncle sam hat toppers

Uncle Sam wants YOU . . . to make these cute little cupcake toppers.
Top your 4th of July cupcakes with mini marshmallow Uncle Sam hats!

12 mini marshmallows
red edible marker
1/2 cup red candy coating wafers
blue sugar sprinkles
12 red candy coating wafers
12 mini frosted cupcakes

Makes **12** *uncle sam hat toppers*

1. Make vertical lines around a mini marshmallow.

2. Melt red candy coating according to package instructions.

3. Slightly dip one end of the marshmallow into the melted candy coating. Place dipped side down on wax or parchment paper to flatten and dry.

4. Then, dip the other end of the marshmallow in the melted candy coating. Immediately place the dipped end into a small bowl of blue sugar sprinkles to coat.

5. Place the red candy coating wafer flat side up and attach the blue sprinkle end of the marshmallow on top of the flat side of the candy coating wafer with the melted candy coating so it resembles a tiny hat.

6. Put the marshmallow hat on top of a mini frosted cupcake.

patriotic rice krispie treat pops

Exploding with cuteness.
Rice Krispie Treat 4th of July pops that won't melt at your patriotic picnic!

12 store-bought Rice Krispie Treat bars
12 popsicle sticks
1 (12-oz.) bag of red candy coating wafers
1 (12-oz.) bag of white candy coating wafers
1 (12-oz.) bag of blue candy coating wafers

Makes **12** patriotic rice krispie treat pops

1. Cut the corners into a curve on one end of the Rice Krispie Treat bar.

2. Melt white candy coating according to package instructions.

3. Dip the Rice Krispie Treat three-fourths of the way into the white candy coating. Lightly tap treat on the edge of the bowl to remove excess. Place on wax or parchment paper. Dry completely.

4. Melt red candy coating according to package instructions.

5. Dip the straight bottom edge of the treat one-third of the way into the melted red candy coating. Lightly tap treat on edge of bowl to remove excess. Place on wax or parchment paper. Dry completely.

6. Melt blue candy coating according to package instructions.

7. Dip the curved top part of the treat one-third of the way into the melted blue candy coating. Lightly tap treat on edge of bowl to remove excess. Place on wax or parchment paper. Dry completely.

8. Push the popsicle stick halfway into the bottom of the treat.

Tip: To make these treats even more adorable, use a black edible marker to draw a smiley face on them!

Sweet Celebrations

Birthdays

bitty balloon cookies

Lofty little cookies to get your celebration started!
Candy-coated Oreos with itty bitty balloons that will make your party pop!

**1 (12-oz.) bag or 1 (16-oz.) bark of
white candy coating**
12 Oreo cookies
M&M candies
primary color confetti sprinkles
black edible marker

Makes **12** *bitty balloon cookies*

1. Melt candy coating according to package instructions

2. Using a fork, dip the Oreo into the melted candy coating. Tap the fork on the side of the bowl to remove excess.

3. Carefully slide the Oreo onto parchment paper.

4. With a toothpick dipped in candy coating, draw a curved white line on top of 2 of the M&M's so they look like balloons.

5. Attach a confetti sprinkle to the bottom of the same color M&M balloon using a toothpick dipped in candy coating.

6. Place the M&M balloons on top of the cookie. Make sure to leave enough room so you can draw in the string.

7. Press confetti sprinkles around the edge of the cookie. Let dry completely.

8. With a black edible marker, draw in squiggly lines on top of the cookie for the balloon strings.

Tip: For step-by step instructions on how to dip Oreos, see page xv.

Sweet Celebrations

circus animal cookie cupcakes

Step right up for a sprinkle-coated birthday treat!
Send in your little clowns to enjoy these easy to make Circus Animal Cookie Cupcakes!

12 circus animal cookies
1/2 cup white candy coating wafers
12 yellow-and-white striped
       candy sticks
pastel-colored Sixlet candies
multicolored nonpareil sprinkles
12 frosted cupcakes

Makes **12** *circus animal cookie cupcakes*

1. Melt white candy coating wafers according to package instructions

2. Attach the circus animal cookie to the front of a candy stick using the melted candy coating. Let dry completely.

3. Dip the top of the candy stick in the melted candy coating. Place a Sixlet on top of the stick and hold until set.

4. Push the stick in the middle of a cupcake.

5. Place the Sixlet candies around the bottom of the stick.

6. Sprinkle the frosting with the multicolored nonpareil sprinkles.

mini celebration cones

A super cool snack.
Scoop up some fun by making Rice Krispie Treat ice cream cones!

12 mini ice cream cones
6 store-bought Rice Krispie Treat bars
1 (12-oz.) bag white candy coating wafers
12 red Sixlet candies
multicolored jimmies sprinkles

Makes **12** *mini celebration cones*

1. Cut Rice Krispie Treat bar in half.

2. Roll one half of the treat into a ball.

3. Melt white candy coating wafers according to package instructions.

4. Dip the rim of the cone into the melted candy coating.

5. Place the Rice Krispie Treat ball on top of the cone and press down to secure. Let dry completely.

6. Turn the cone upside down and dip the Rice Krispie Treat all the way into the white melted candy coating. Lightly tap on side of the bowl to remove excess candy coating,

7. Set cone down and immediately place a red Sixlet candy on top.

8. Sprinkle the multicolored jimmies on top. Let dry completely.

Graduation

diploma cupcake toppers

Sweet little certificates to top your grad party cupcakes!
It's easy to make dozens of diplomas with store-bought rolled fondant!

Approximately 3 oz. store-bought white rolled fondant
fondant rolling pin
1¹/₂-inch circle cookie or fondant cutter
1 (.68-oz.) red writing icing tube (not gel)

Makes **12** diploma cupcake toppers

1. Roll fondant flat to approximately ⅛-inch thickness.

2. Using the circle cookie cutter, cut circle shape out of the fondant.

3. Starting at one edge of the circle, roll the fondant to the other end.

4. Lightly squeeze the middle and gently pull on each end to elongate so it resembles a diploma.

5. With the red writing icing, pipe on a small red bow in the middle of the diploma.

6. Let dry overnight.

7. Place on top of frosted cupcake.

happy graduate cake pops

Hats off to these cute cake pops!
These will earn you a degree in adorableness.

12 snack cakes (such as Little Debbie Fancy Cakes)
1 (12-oz.) bag of yellow candy coating wafers
12 lollipop sticks
12 chocolate squares (such as Ghirardelli or World Market)
12 Mini M&M's
1 Fruit by the Foot
12 miniature peanut butter cups
black edible marker

Makes **12** *happy graduate cake pops*

1. Unwrap 1 snack cake and place in a bowl. Mash with a fork or mush with your hands to bind the frosting and cake together.

2. Roll into a ball.

3. Melt candy coating wafers according to package instructions.

4. Dip one end of a lollipop stick in the melted candy coating and push halfway into the cake ball.

5. Place cake pops on a cookie sheet lined with parchment paper in the freezer for an hour.

6. Dip cake pop into the melted candy coating, tapping the stick gently against the side of the bowl to remove excess.

7. Place in Styrofoam block to dry.

8. Cut off a 2-inch strip of Fruit by the Foot, then cut in half horizontally.

9. Make 3 cuts lengthwise halfway through the Fruit by the Foot.

10. Roll the remaining uncut part of the Fruit by the Foot together so it resembles a tassel.

11. Attach the tassel to the middle of the chocolate square with the melted candy coating.

12. With a toothpick dipped in melted candy coating, attach the Mini M&M in the middle of the chocolate square and cover the tassel. Let dry completely.

13. Using the melted candy coating, attach the chocolate square to the BOTTOM of a miniature peanut butter cup so it resembles the mortarboard cap.

14. Secure the cap to the top of the cake pop using the melted candy coating.

15. With the black edible marker, draw a smiley face on the front of the cake pop.

Tip: For step-by step instructions on how to make no-bake cake pops, see page xvii.

delicious diplomas

Making these tasty treats will move you to the head of the class!
You'll get an A+ from your graduate when they see an edible diploma from their alma mater.

6 toaster pastries
1 (7-oz.) pouch white cookie icing
red Fruit Roll-Up
yellow jumbo flower sprinkle
edible black marker

Makes **6** delicious diplomas

1. Flip toaster pastry over and spread with white cookie icing.

2. Let dry and harden completely (approximately 24 hours).

3. Using a small circle cookie cutter or pastry tip, cut a circle out of a red Fruit Roll-Up.

4. Cut 2 small strips (approximately 1½ inches long) of the fruit roll up for the ribbon.

5. Attach the 2 Fruit Roll-Up ribbons to the back of the circle Fruit Roll-Up using the cookie icing.

6. Secure the yellow jumbo flower sprinkle to the middle of the Fruit Roll-Up circle with cookie icing.

7. Using a small amount of cookie icing, attach the ribbon to the bottom corner of the toaster pastry.

8. Write the word "DIPLOMA" using the black edible marker on the top of the toaster pastry.

9. You can personalize the diploma with the graduate's name and the date of the ceremony if you wish.

Bridal Shower

bridal shower umbrella pops

Shower the bride-to-be with cuteness.
Pretty parasol pops made with mini meringue cookies.

**1 (12-oz.) bag lilac candy coating
      wafers (or any color to match
      your bridal shower)**
24 lollipop sticks
24 mini store-bought meringue cookies
white pearl nonpareil sprinkles

Makes **24** *bridal shower
umbrella pops*

1. Melt candy coating wafers according to package instructions.

2. Dip one end of a lollipop stick into the melted candy coating and push into bottom center of the meringue cookie. Let dry.

3. Holding the stick, dip the meringue cookie into the melted candy coating.

4. Gently tap the stick on the side of the bowl to remove excess coating.

5. Push stick in Styrofoam block.

6. Place a white pearl nonpareil sprinkle at the end of each ridge of the cookie. Hold in place until set.

sweet bride cookie

An adorable cookie for the blushing bride.
A meringue cookie all dressed up for the special day!

1 store-bought meringue cookie (such as Trader Joe's)
1/2 cup white candy coating wafers
1 white chocolate truffle
black edible marker
9 white pearl candies
1 white jumbo flower sprinkle
white pearl nonpareil sprinkles

Makes 1 sweet bride cookie

1. With a knife, make a small slice off the top of the meringue cookie so the top is flat.

2. Melt white candy coating according to package instructions.

3. Attach the white chocolate truffle to the top flat part of the meringue cookie.

4. Draw a smiley face on the white chocolate truffle with a black edible marker.

5. Using a toothpick dipped in white melted candy coating, attach the white pearl candies around the neck of the bride cookie.

6. Attach white pearl nonpareil sprinkles to the meringue cookie in a random pattern for the dress, using a toothpick dipped in the melted candy coating.

7. With a toothpick dipped in melted candy coating, attach a white pearl nonpareil sprinkle to the center of the jumbo white flower sprinkle. Attach with melted candy coating to the head of the bride cookie.

Tip: For a fun twist, switch out the pearl and sprinkle colors to match the color of the brides-maids' dresses. Then use food coloring mist to spray the meringue cookies to make bridesmaid cookies. Makes a fun shower favor!

mini wedding cake

Sweet and petite.
This elegant little no-bake wedding cake is perfect for your bridal shower!

1 (10.75-oz.) frozen pound cake (such as Sara Lee)
1/2-inch circle cookie cutter
1 1/2-inch circle cookie cutter
2-inch circle cookie cutter
1/2 cup white candy coating wafers
white pearl candies
white pearl nonpareil sprinkles
white heart sprinkles
1 jumbo white flower sprinkle
1 jumbo white heart sprinkle

Makes **1** mini wedding cake

1. Cut the frozen pound cake into slices that are approximately ¾-inch thick.

2. With the cookie cutters, cut out the 3 differently sized circles.

3. Melt candy coating according to package instructions.

4. Attach white pearl candies around the bottom of the largest circle with the melted candy coating.

5. Place the 1½-inch pound cake circle on top of the 2-inch circle. Secure with melted candy coating.

6. Attach white pearl nonpareil sprinkles around the bottom of the 2nd tier of the cake.

7. Place the ½-inch cake on top of the 2nd tier. Secure with melted candy coating.

8. Attach white pearl nonpareil sprinkles around the bottom of the top tier.

9. Attach white heart sprinkles to the cake using a toothpick dipped in melted white candy coating.

10. Attach white jumbo flower sprinkle to the top of the cake with melted candy coating.

11. Place a white pearl nonpareil sprinkle in the center of the white jumbo heart sprinkle with a toothpick dipped in melted candy coating.

12. Secure the heart sprinkle to the top of the cake using melted candy coating. Hold in place until set.

Bachelorette Party

pretzel bling ring

Put a ring on it.
Put a super sweet engagement ring on top of Oreos.

**1 package of Snackwell's 100-calorie
    Round Yogurt Pretzels
1 (1.5-oz.) can silver mist food coloring
    spray
1/2 cup white candy coating wafers
10 white gumdrops
10 Oreos**

**Makes approximately 10
pretzel bling rings**

1. Spread out the round yogurt-covered pretzels on parchment or wax paper.

2. Using the silver food coloring mist, spray the pretzels. Let dry completely.

3. Turn and spray the other side of the pretzels. Let dry completely.

4. Melt candy coating wafers according to package instructions.

5. Dip the top of a white gumdrop in the melted candy coating.

6. Place on top of the pretzel ring and hold until set.

7. Twist off the top of an Oreo and eat it.

8. Push down the pretzel ring in the cream filling part of the other half of the Oreo so it stands up on its own.

Sweet Celebrations

kissy cakes

Top a store-bought snack cake with a sweet smooch!
You'll only need 2 ingredients to create this kissable cake!

1 (12-oz.) bag of bright pink candy
     coating wafers
1 lip candy mold
8 Little Debbie Zebra Snack Cakes

Makes **8** kissy cakes

1. Melt candy coating wafers according to package instructions,

2. Fill lip candy mold with melted candy coating using a spoon, squeeze bottle, or plastic decorating bag.

3. Tap mold gently on the counter a few times to eliminate air bubbles.

4. Place mold in refrigerator until the underside of the mold looks frosty and the candy is set.

5. To remove candy from mold, place mold upside down over parchment paper and gently flex the mold.

6. With a little melted candy coating or white frosting, attach the candy lips to the top of the Little Debbie Zebra Snack Cakes.

Tip: Lip candy molds can be purchased at Michael's stores or online.

teeny martini cupcake toppers

...etty in pink.
Cute little cosmo cupcake toppers to celebrate girls' night out!

Cox

1/2 cup white candy coating wafers
12 Hershey's Hugs candies
pink sugar sprinkles
4 lollipop sticks
12 white candy coating wafers
12 frosted cupcakes

Makes **12** teeny martini cupcake toppers

1. Melt candy coating according to package instructions

2. With a toothpick dipped in melted candy coating, draw a rim around the bottom of the Hershey's Hug.

3. Immediately cover the rim with pink sugar sprinkles. Let dry completely.

4. Cut lollipop stick in 1-inch sections.

5. Cut the tip off of the Hershey's Hug so that it stands flat.

6. Dip one end of the lollipop stick into the candy coating and place on the flat tip of the Hershey's Hug. Hold until set.

7. Dip the other end of the lollipop stick into the melted candy coating and place in the middle of the white candy coating wafer. Hold until set.

8. Place the teeny martini on top of a frosted cupcake.

Baby Shower

ducky cookies

Splish splash! A perfect cookie for your baby shower bash!
Bubbling with cuteness, this cookie is just ducky.

1 (16-oz.) can white frosting
blue food coloring
12 store-bought sugar cookies
optional: 1 French decorating tip (Wilton 4B) and piping bag
1 (16-oz.) frozen pound cake (such as Sara Lee)
mini duck cookie cutter (1^1/$_2$-inch)
white Sixlet candies
white pearl candies
orange edible marker
black nonpareil pearl sprinkle

Makes **12** ducky cookies

1. Mix 5 drops of blue food coloring in the can of white frosting. Add more food coloring for a darker blue.

2. Using a large French decorating tip (Wilton 8B), pipe frosting on top of the cookie, or simply spread the frosting on the cookie with a knife.

3. Cut frozen pound cake into slices 1-inch thick.

4. With the mini duck cookie cutter, cut duck shapes out of the pound cake.

5. Press in the black nonpareil pearl sprinkle into the duck cake for the eye.

6. Using the orange edible marker, color in the beak of the duck.

7. Set pound cake duck upright in the frosting on top of the cookie.

8. Place white Sixlet candies and pearl nonpareils in frosting to resemble bubbles.

Tip: For step-by-step instructions on how to pipe frosting, see page xvi.

baby bedtime bears

Nummy little nappers perfect for your party!
You'll want to tuck away these little baby bear cookies!

6 pink sugar wafer cookies
6 chocolate sugar wafer cookies
6 vanilla flavored Tootsie Rolls
6 blue raspberry Jolly Rancher Chews
24 Honey Teddy Grahams
1/2 cup white candy coating wafers
12 white heart sprinkles
12 pink heart sprinkles
black edible marker

Makes 24 baby bedtime bears

1. Cut sugar wafer cookies in half.

2. Microwave Tootsie Rolls and Jolly Rancher Chews for approximately 7 seconds to soften.

3. Roll out the candy and cut into 1-inch squares.

4. Melt candy coating wafers according to package instructions.

5. Attach Teddy Grahams to the wafer cookies with the melted candy coating.

6. Place the white candy blankets over the bears on top of the pink sugar wafer cookies.

7. Place the blue candy blankets over the bears on top of the chocolate sugar wafer cookies.

8. Using a toothpick dipped in melted candy coating, attach the white heart sprinkles to the middle of the blue blankets and the pink heart sprinkles on the white blankets.

9. Draw in the eyes and noses on the Teddy Grahams with a black edible marker.

twinkie toes

Sweet feet.
Yummy little baby bootie cakes made on a shoestring budget!

Cox

12 Hostess Twinkie Snack Cakes
12 Golden Oreos
1 (16-oz.) can white frosting
premade yellow royal icing flowers
green licorice lace (such as Rips Whips)

Makes **6** pairs of twinkie toes

1. Slice off one curved end of the Twinkie.

2. With frosting, attach a Golden Oreo to the top of the Twinkie towards the cut end.

3. Attach the icing flower to the front of the Golden Oreo with frosting.

4. Tie bows using the licorice lace. Secure to top of Twinkie with frosting

Tip: Make the laces just before serving. The bows may dry and break in half if they are made too far in advance.

Just for Fun

Fiesta

sombrero sponge cake

Nacho average sombrero.
A sweet sombrero made from store-bought snack and sponge cakes!

1 Hostess Twinkie snack cake
1 sponge cake dessert cup
1 red Fruit Roll-Up
1 (.68-oz.) tube red writing icing
(not gel)
Skittles candies

Makes 1 sombrero sponge cake

1. Cut Twinkie in half.

2. Put Twinkie cut side down inside of the sponge cake cup.

3. Cut a Fruit Roll-Up strip and wrap around the bottom of the Twinkie.

4. With the writing icing, decorate the side of the sponge cake cup and attach Skittles to the bottom of the cup.

Tip: These taste great with a little strawberry sauce and whipped cream on top!

piñata rice krispie treat

The sweetest party animal.
Fun fiesta food that is sure to be a big hit!

2 store-bought Rice Krispie Treat bars
1 (16-oz.) can white frosting
1 cup sweetened shredded coconut
blue food coloring gel
purple food coloring gel
yellow food coloring gel
pink food coloring gel
orange food coloring gel
1 candy eye
6 candy corns

Makes **1** *piñata rice krispie treat*

1. Using a knife, cut off about one-third of 1 Rice Krispie Treat bar. Cut off the corners at one end for the piñata head.

2. Attach the head to the end of the other Rice Krispie Treat with frosting.

3. Spread frosting on top of the Rice Krispie Treats.

4. Divide coconut into 5 plastic zipper bags.

5. Place a small amount of food coloring gel in the bag. Place a different color in each bag. A little goes a long way.

6. Knead gel into the coconut to incorporate.

7. Starting with the pink coconut, press one row on the top of the piñata head. Continue to add rows with the remaining colors.

8. Place a small amount of frosting on the back of the candy eye and place on the piñata head.

9. Attach 2 candy corns with frosting for the ears to the top of the head.

10. Turn 4 candy corns upside down and attach with frosting for the legs.

Tip: To achieve the bright colors on the coconut, use food coloring gel found at your local craft stores.

taco cupcakes

So cute, everyone will taco-bout them.
Fondant tacos stuffed with all things sweet!

3 oz. yellow fondant
Small 1¹/₂-inch circle cookie or fondant
    cutter
Chocolate snack cake or cookie
1 orange circus peanut candy
¹/₄ cup sweetened shredded coconut
green food coloring
12 frosted cupcakes

Makes **12** taco cupcakes

1. Roll out fondant to approximately ⅛-inch thickness.

2. Cut circles out of the fondant with the cookie cutter.

3. Bend the circle in half so it resembles a taco shell.

4. Crumble the chocolate snack cake or cookie and sprinkle a few crumbs inside the shell for the meat.

5. Cut up the orange circus peanut candy in small pieces and place a few on top of the taco meat for the cheese.

6. Put the coconut in a plastic zipper bag with a drop of green food coloring and shake. Sprinkle a few pieces inside the taco for the lettuce.

7. Place taco on top of a frosted cupcake.

Just for Fun

Summer Fun

sandy beach cupcakes

So flippin' cute!
Topped with teeny tiny candy flip flops, these beachy cupcakes are a shore thing!

12 cupcakes, unfrosted
1 (16-oz.) can white frosting
1 cup brown sugar
24 Pez candies
24 flower sprinkles
12 green gumdrops
1 small 1¹/₂-inch daisy cookie cutter
12 pretzels sticks

Makes **12** sandy beach cupcakes

1. Lightly frost the top of the cupcake.

2. Pour the brown sugar in a bowl.

3. Holding the cupcake upside down, press the frosted side into the brown sugar so it is completely covered.

4. With a toothpick dipped in frosting, attach the flower sprinkles to one end of the Pez candies so they resemble flip flops.

5. Put a green gumdrop in between 2 pieces of parchment paper and roll flat with rolling pin.

6. Using the daisy cookie cutter, cut a flower shape out of the rolled green gumdrop.

7. Attach the middle of the daisy gumdrop to one end of the pretzel stick with frosting so it resembles a palm tree.

8. Place the palm tree and flip flops on top of the cupcake.

Tip: Don't have a daisy cookie cutter? Use a small circle cookie cutter instead and then cut small "V" shapes around the edge of the circle.

shark marshmallow pops

They're Jaws-ome.
These sweet sharks were inspired by a real shark—Barbara Corcoran, the star of the television show "Shark Tank." But she's really not a shark, no sir; she's one of the nicest people on the planet. She believed in a little guppy like me and was sweet enough to endorse both of my books. She's totally fin-tastic!

12 regular-size marshmallows
1 (1.5-oz.) can silver mist food coloring spray
red sugar sprinkles
1/2 cup white candy coating wafers
3 black Necco wafer candies
24 candy eyes
12 Baby Goldfish crackers
12 lollipop sticks

Makes 12 shark marshmallow pops

1. Lightly spray marshmallow with silver food coloring mist.

2. With kitchen shears, make a cut one-third of the way down from the top of the marshmallow that goes three-fourths of the way into the marshmallow for the mouth. Be careful that the cut does not go all of the way through.

3. Pour red sugar sprinkles onto a shallow plate. Carefully open the mouth and press the cut sides down into the red sprinkles to coat the inside.

4. Melt white candy coating wafers according to package instructions

5. Cut the black Necco wafer candy into quarters, first in half and then again in half, for the fins. These may break when cutting, so you may need to keep a few more black ones on hand.

6. Attach Necco wafer fin to the back of the shark pop with melted candy coating.

7. With a toothpick dipped in candy coating, secure 2 of the candy eyes to the top of the shark pop.

8. Place a small amount of melted candy coating on one side of a Baby Goldfish cracker and place inside the shark's mouth.

9. Push a lollipop stick into the bottom of the shark marshmallow.

Tip: Dip the kitchen scissors into water to prevent sticking when cutting marshmallows.

popsicle cupcakes

Super cool.
Itty bitty candy popsicles so cute they'll make your heart melt.

24 Mike and Ike candies
24 Flat toothpicks
12 frosted cupcakes

Makes **12** popsicle cupcakes

1. Cut toothpicks in half.

2. Push toothpick into the bottom of the candy so the wide flat end sticks out. It may be easier to push the toothpick in the candy if you start a hole using a pointy toothpick or wooden skewer.

3. Place on top of frosted cupcake.

Tip: If serving to small children, please take the toothpicks out first!

teddy pool krispies

Dive into some beary yummy treats.
Make a splash with the kids! They will love creating their own sweet swimming snacks!

12 store-bought Rice Krispie Treats
1 (16-oz.) can of white frosting
blue food coloring
orange and yellow Mini M&M's
Gummy Lifesavers, gumballs, and Rips
    candy in bite-size pieces
Honey Teddy Grahams
paper drink umbrellas
black edible marker

Cox

Makes 12 teddy pool krispies

1. Mix the blue food coloring in the can of white frosting until you get the desired blue color.

2. Frost the top of the Rice Krispie Treat.

3. Alternate the orange and yellow mini M&M's around the outside of the Rice Krispie Treat to form the pool.

4. Put a Gummy Lifesaver candy in the middle of the pool. Cut the Teddy Graham in half and attach to the top of the Lifesaver with frosting.

5. Make 2 more Rice Krispie Treat pools. On one of the pools put 2 Teddy Grahams that have been cut in half in the pool with a gumball. For the other pool place a bite-size Rips candy in the pool and lay a Teddy Graham on top.

6. Push in paper drink umbrellas in the pool.

7. Using the black edible marker, draw in eyes and noses on the Teddy Grahams.

snow cone cake pops

Sweeten your summer with these shimmery Snow Cone Cake Pops.
These icy treats won't melt on a hot summer's day, and you'll stay cool in the kitchen because they are no-bake cake pops!

12 snack cakes (such as Little Debbie Fancy Cakes)
1 (12-oz.) bag of white candy coating wafers
12 lollipop sticks
colored sugar sprinkles
white paper
tape or glue stick

Makes **12** *snow cone cake pops*

1. Unwrap 1 snack cake and place in a bowl. Mash with a fork or mush with your hands to bind the frosting and cake together.

2. Roll into a ball.

3. Melt candy coating wafers according to package instructions.

4. Dip one end of a lollipop stick in the melted candy coating and push halfway into the cake ball.

5. Place cake pops on a cookie sheet lined with parchment paper in the freezer for an hour.

6. Dip cake pop into the melted candy coating, tapping the stick gently against the side of the bowl to remove excess.

7. Immediately pour sugar sprinkles over the cake pop to coat. Hold the cake pop over a small bowl to catch the excess to reuse.

8. Cut a 4-inch circle out of white paper. Cut the circle in half and wrap it around the bottom of the cake pop. Tape or glue ends together to secure.

9. Repeat using different colored sugar sprinkles if desired.

Tip: For step-by step instructions on how to make no-bake cake pops, see page xvii.

Game Night

peanut butter checkers

Everyone's game for candy-coated checkers!
Yummy game pieces made from peanut butter–filled crackers.

1 (12-oz.) bag red candy coating wafers
1 (12-oz.) bag dark chocolate candy coating wafers
1 (7.5-oz.) box peanut butter-filled Ritz Bits crackers

Makes **1** entire box of peanut butter cookies

1. Melt red and dark chocolate candy coating wafers separately according to package instructions.

2. Place peanut butter Ritz Bits cracker on top of a fork and dip into the melted candy coating, covering the entire cracker.

3. Lift the cracker out with fork and tap fork against bowl to remove excess.

4. Carefully slide cracker off the fork onto wax or parchment paper.

5. Let dry completely.

6. For the game, make 12 red and 12 black checkers.

Tip: These are awesome—and I mean AWESOME—refrigerated.

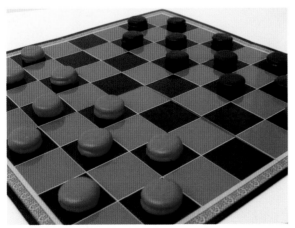

twister graham crackers

A fun twist on everyone's favorite game!
Graham crackers, icing, and candy put a new spin on a family classic!

4 graham crackers
1 (7-oz.) pouch white cookie icing
blue, green, red, and yellow Mini M&M's
red edible marker

Makes **4** *twister graham crackers*

1. Frost the top of the graham cracker with white cookie icing.

2. Leaving approximately ¼-inch on each end, place 6 green Mini M&M's across the graham cracker to make a row. Then, continue to make rows of 6 using the yellow, blue, and finally the red Mini M&M's to resemble the Twister mat.

3. Let dry 24 hours.

4. Write the word "Twister" at each end of the graham cracker using a red edible marker.

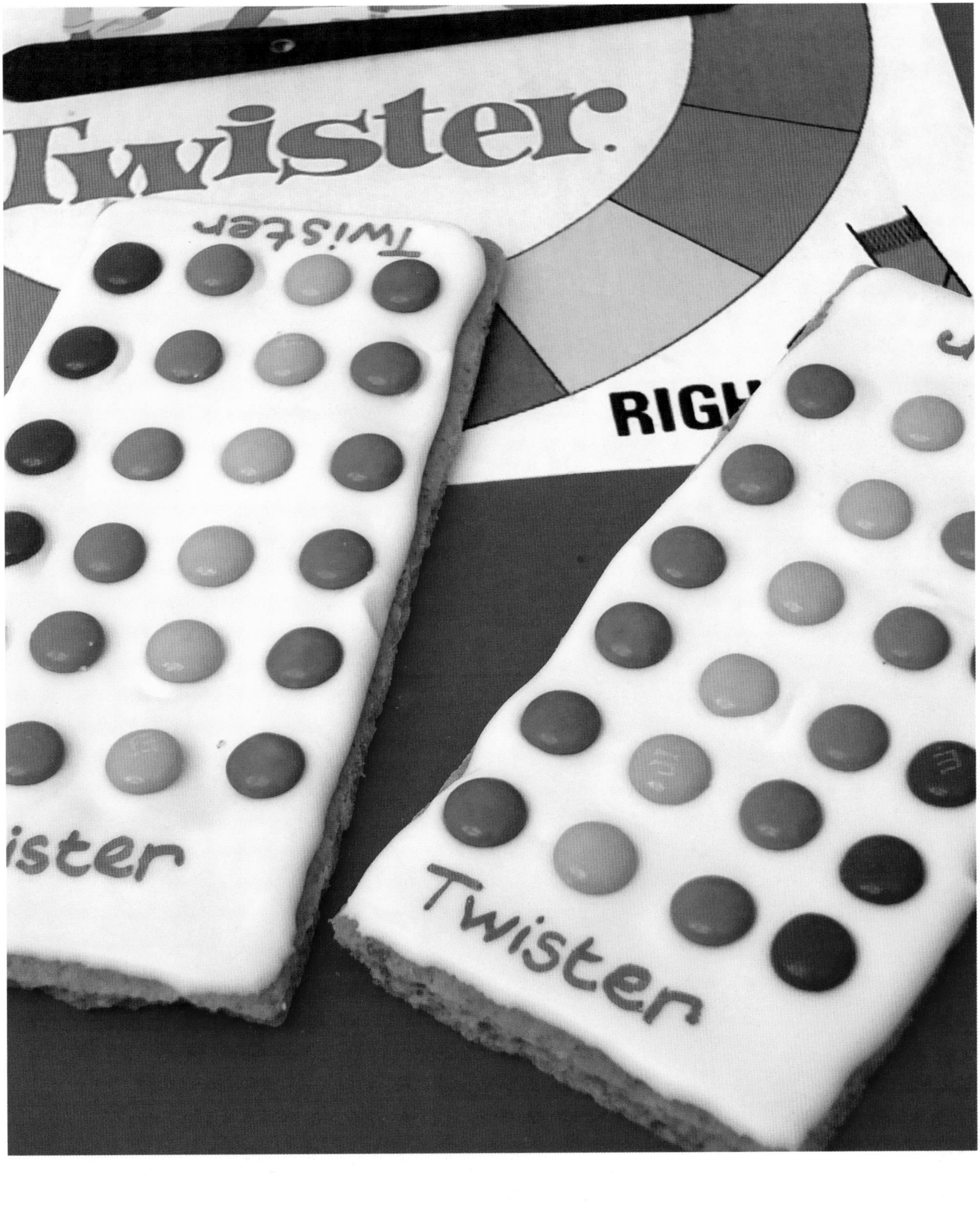
Twister.
Twister
Twister
RIGH

toaster pastry cards

They're kind of a big deal.
Go all in for the treat that's all decked out.

4 toaster pastries
1 (7-oz.) pouch of white cookie icing
red edible marker
black edible marker

Makes **4** toaster pastry cards

1. Flip toaster pastry over and spread with white cookie icing.

2. Let dry for 24 hours.

3. With an edible marker, draw the card faces on the icing.

Just for Fun

domino rice krispie treat

Set up some fun with a domino dessert!
These treats are spot on with unmatched cuteness!

12 store-bought Rice Krispie Treat bars
1 (16-oz.) can white frosting
3 Tootsie Rolls
brown M&M's

Makes **12** *domino rice krispie treats*

1. Spread the top of a Rice Krispie Treat with white frosting.

2. Soften Tootsie Roll microwave for approximately 7 seconds.

3. Roll Tootsie Roll into a thin rope.

4. Cut Tootsie Roll rope to fit across the Rice Krispie Treat horizontally.

5. Place the rope in the middle of the Rice Krispie Treat.

6. Put the brown M&M's in a domino pattern on the Rice Krispie Treat.

Tip: Don't have M&M's? Use chocolate chips turned upside down!

pound cake dice pops

Start your game night rolling with delicious dice cake pops!
An easy-to-make treat that is a sure bet!

1 (16-oz.) frozen pound cake (such as
Sara Lee)
1 (12-oz.) bag white candy coating
wafers
10 lollipop sticks
black confetti sprinkles

Makes approximately **10** pound
cake dice pops

1. Cut pound cake into 1½-inch cubes.

2. Dip one end of a lollipop stick into the melted candy coating and push halfway into the top of a cake cube. Freeze for 15 minutes.

3. Holding the lollipop stick, dip the cake cube into the melted candy coating and tap the stick on the side of the bowl to remove the excess.

4. Place on parchment paper to dry.

5. With a toothpick dipped in melted candy coating, apply the black confetti sprinkles in a dice pattern.

Tip: It may be easier to cut and dip the pound cake while still frozen.

Sports

basketball cookies

Pass the milk for a slam dunk.
Score big with your team of hoopsters when you create these super easy cookies!

30 vanilla wafer cookies
**1 (1.5-oz.) can orange mist food coloring
    spray**
black edible marker

Makes **30** basketball cookies

1. Place vanilla wafers on wax or parchment paper.

2. Spray the cookies with orange food coloring spray. Let dry completely.

3. Draw on lines with a black edible marker so the cookies resemble a basketball.

Tip: Spread frosting in between 2 cookies and add a lollipop stick for cookie pops!

Just for Fun

football pretzels

Are you ready for some FOOTBALL!?
Hershey's Hugs + Pretzels + Almonds = TOUCHDOWN!

50 raw or roasted almonds
50 Hershey's Hugs
50 square pretzel waffles
black edible marker

Makes **50** *football pretzels*

1. Using the black edible marker, draw 2 lines on each end of an almond. Then draw one small line in the middle of the almond and 3 tiny lines crossing the small line to resemble laces.

2. Unwrap the Hershey's Hugs and place on top of the square pretzel waffle.

3. Preheat oven to 250 degrees.

4. Place pretzel topped Hershey's Hugs on a cookie sheet lined with parchment paper and put in the oven for approximately 4 minutes (until soft but not melted).

5. Remove from oven after 4 minutes, place football almond on top, and gently press down.

6. Place tray into refrigerator for 20 minutes to set.

Tip: You can use regular Hershey's Kisses, but the melted Hershey's Hugs look like referee uniforms!

baseball field graham crackers

A graham slam.
You'll knock one out of the park when you make these with the kiddos! These ball game treats are sure to be a home run!

1 (16-oz.) can white frosting
green food coloring
10 graham cracker squares
10 white Necco wafer candies
red edible marker
40 white Chiclets

Makes **10** baseball field graham crackers

1. Add green food coloring into a can of white frosting and stir to incorporate. Add more drops of food coloring to achieve your desired green color.

2. Spread green frosting on graham cracker square.

3. Draw stitching using a red edible marker on the white Necco wafer candy so it resembles a baseball.

4. Place baseball Necco wafer in the center of the frosted graham cracker.

5. Place 4 white Chiclets on each corner of the graham cracker for bases.

golf donuts

Literally a hole-in-one.
Make these tee-rific treats fore your favorite golfer!

12 mini donuts
1 (16-oz.) can vanilla frosting
$^1/_2$ cup sweetened shredded coconut
green food coloring
red Fruit by the Foot
12 pretzel sticks
12 white Sixlet candies

Makes **12** golf donuts

1. Spread frosting on top of donut.

2. Place coconut in plastic zipper bag and add food coloring until you get the desired green grass color.

3. Press green coconut on top of the frosted donut.

4. Using kitchen shears, cut a small triangle out of the red Fruit by the Foot for the golf flag.

5. Attach flag to one end of a pretzel stick with frosting.

6. Press flag stick into the center of the donut.

7. Place a white Sixlet candy next to the flag-stick for the golf ball.

Tip: Chocolate donuts make these taste like candy bars!

Just for Fun

Camping

oreo bear cookies

Beary sweet.
Use store-bought cookies to create a treat everyone will love, fur sure!

12 Oreo cookies
12 Mini Nilla wafer cookies
1 (16-oz.) can of chocolate frosting
12 mini black jelly beans
black edible marker
24 dark brown M&M's
24 candy eyes

Makes **12** oreo bear cookies

1. Spread chocolate frosting on the back of a Mini Nilla wafer cookie and place on the Oreo towards the bottom.

2. Attach the mini black jelly bean to the Mini Nilla wafer with frosting.

3. Draw the mouth on the Mini Nilla wafer under the nose with a black edible marker.

4. With frosting, attach 2 dark brown M&M's to the top of the Oreo for the ears.

5. Secure the candy eyes on the Oreo with frosting.

fishing dock treat

No trout about it, this snack is a reel catch.
A crafty little treat for your camping trip that's so cute it should be gillegal.

1 graham cracker
1 (16-oz.) can white frosting
blue food coloring
1 Kit Kat bar
3 Tootsie Rolls
1 white Airhead candy
1 green gumdrop
2 toothpicks
2 Baby Goldfish crackers

Makes 1 fishing dock treat

1. Tint the can of white frosting with blue food coloring. Add the food coloring and mix until the desired color is achieved.

2. Spread frosting on top of graham cracker.

3. Break off 1 piece of the Kit Kat bar.

4. Cut 2 Tootsie Rolls in half. Attach the half to each end of the Kit Kat for the fishing dock. Place dock at one end of the frosted graham cracker.

5. Flatten out the green gumdrop a little and with kitchen shears cut into 4 pointy strips to resemble leaves.

6. Soften a Tootsie Roll in the microwave for approximately 7 seconds. Break off a small piece and shape into an oval so it resembles a reed.

7. Place Tootsie Roll reed on the end of a toothpick.

8. Push the toothpick in between 2 gumdrop leaves.

9. Place reed next to dock.

10. Break off a small piece of the white Airhead candy. Roll into a thin rope for the fishing line.

11. Tie the Airhead fishing line to one end of a pretzel stick. At the other end of the line, attach a Baby Goldfish cracker with frosting.

12. Cut a Baby Goldfish in half and put the head sticking out of the frosting.

s'more cupcake toppers

Make lots of these little guys because everyone will be asking for s'more.
Tiny treats with a big s'more taste. Easy to make from cereal, marshmallows, and frosting; create them at the campsite or at home, they're s'moredorable anywhere!

12 mini marshmallows
black edible marker
1 (16-oz.) can chocolate frosting
24 Golden Graham cereal squares

Makes **12** s'more cupcake toppers

1. Using the black edible marker, draw a smiley face on a mini marshmallow.

2. Spread frosting over 1 Golden Graham cereal square.

3. Place the mini marshmallow on top of the frosted cereal square.

4. Put a small amount of frosting on the top of the mini marshmallow.

5. Place another golden graham cereal square on top of the mini marshmallow.

6. Set the cute little s'more on top of a mini cupcake.

Just for Fun

nutter butter campers

They're tentastic.
Sweet and cute cookies that are perfect for a camping party, to take along to your campsite, or any time you want a sleepy little snack! So adorable, it's in-tents.

2 Nutter Butter cookies
1 (16-oz.) can chocolate frosting
2 Mini Nilla wafers
1 green Fruit Roll-Up
black edible marker
1 Oreo cookie
3 pretzel sticks
1 orange gumdrop
1 yellow gumdrop
1 red gumdrop
optional: Graham Crackers for tents

Makes **2** *nutter butter campers,*
1 *oreo campfire, and*
1 *graham cracker tent*

1. Attach the Mini Nilla wafer to the top of a Nutter Butter cookie with frosting.

2. Draw on a sleeping face onto the Mini Nilla wafer cookie with a black edible marker.

3. With kitchen shears, cut a green Fruit Roll-Up to fit around the bottom of the Nutter Butter cookie. Wrap the Fruit Roll-Up around the cookie.

4. Spread frosting on top of the Oreo.

5. Snap the pretzels sticks in half and place on top of the Oreo for the firewood.

6. Using kitchen shears, cut the gumdrops into pointy strips.

7. Place gumdrop strips into the frosting for the campfire.

8. Frost the ends of 2 graham crackers together at an angle for the tent.

Tip: Great for sleepover parties too!

Index

135

Index

acknowledgments

Thank you to my sweet hubby Travis for your amazing support. There is no way I could have written this book without your encouragement. Thanks for not flinching when I asked you to go to the party store and for being so willing to haul the Easter boxes down from the garage rafters in August. Thanks mostly for kidnapping me and whisking me off to Vegas again when I was working way too much. I love you more and more each day and I am so honored and proud to be your wife.

To my not-so-little boys, Austin and Carson, thanks for asking if any cookies or treats on the kitchen counter were "fair game" before you ate them. I am grateful for all of your encouragement and help, for doing dishes when I was up to my eyeballs in frosting and for picking up the vacuum when I was busy editing pictures. Mostly, thank you for making me laugh, telling me to take a break, and giving me that much-needed hug. To hear you both say that you are proud of me, well, I can't even begin to tell you how that makes a mom feel. I love you both more than words can say. Yes, even more than chocolate.

Thank you, Mom, for being my biggest cheerleader, for talking to me every day, and for being a shoulder to cry on. You are an itty bitty lady, but you have the biggest heart in the world.

Dad, I know that you were with me every step of the way when I was writing this book. I miss your jokes and your big bear hugs, and I think of you every time I eat ice cream. Especially banana splits.

To all of the sweet fans of Party Pinching, I wouldn't have been able to do any of this without you. I can't tell you how much I appreciate all of the kindness you have shown me over the years. Your emails, photos and comments constantly motivate me to create more cute and fun food! Thank you for faithfully following what's happening on my website, partypinching.com, and on Facebook, Twitter, Pinterest, and Instagram. You are such kind and caring people, and your support means the world to me!

From a young age, my incredible family has instilled in me the love of inhaling sweet desserts and Korean food like there is no tomorrow. I thank you all not only for encouraging/enabling me to experience the joy of pigging out, but for your praise and help throughout this whole process. I feel so fortunate to have such amazing support from my entire family. I wish I could find the words to tell you how much I love and appreciate you all.

To my sweet friends, thank you for rallying around me and for always being there for me.

One of the biggest blessings in my life is to have friends that I can count on. Thanks to all who happily share my work on social media! I am forever grateful and sincerely thankful for every one of you.

It's an honor to be surrounded by such an amazing group of ladies in the blogging community. You are the most creative, generous, and genuine group of people I have had the privilege to know. Even though I haven't met most of you, I thank you for treating me like one of the family and for your inspiration both personally and professionally.

A heartfelt thank-you to Hannah Ballard, Rebekah Claussen, Justin Greer, Lauren Error, Rodney Fife, Meagan Piiparinen, and the entire Cedar Fort Publishing team. You are all a delight to work with and I am in awe of the vision you have for my work. Thank you for believing in me, for your guidance, and for all of your hard work.

Thank you to the sweetest beagle in the world and my partner in cookie crime. Kurby, you never leave my side, you always know when I need a snuggle or tail wag, and you simply make my world a better place. Plus, you never judge me when I sneak a cookie or two or three or four or . . .

about the author

When Norene's sons became teenagers, she realized how much she missed being a room mom. Making sweet treats with the kids and throwing classroom parties were all a thing of the past. As a result, she created Party Pinching, a popular website where she could blog about her cute food and budget-friendly party ideas. Her adorable desserts have been featured in *Family Fun* magazine, *Seventeen* magazine, and *Taste of Home*, and have been praised by Martha Stewart and *Shark Tank*'s Barbara Corcoran. She is a frequent guest on New Day Northwest, a morning television show in Seattle, where her easy dessert demonstrations get rave reviews.

Norene's love for celebrating special occasions with all things sweet inspired her to write *Party with Sweet Treats*, the perfect sequel to her first book, *Sweet Treats for the Holidays*.

Norene lives in the Seattle area with her husband, two sons, and a beagle.

Visit Norene's website, Party Pinching, at www.partypinching.com